mosaic of my mind:

a collection of poetry past, present, and possible

Melissa Moy

ISBN: 1986340775

ISBN-13: 978-1986340779

DEDICATION

for my family, imperfectly my own

for my students, more my children than they will ever understand or know

CONTENTS

ACKNOWLEDGMENTS

I owe great thanks to my students. They always believe in me so deeply and so true. Without their encouragement and support I don't know that I would ever have pushed myself to pursue my passions. Their watchful eyes keep me in check and remind me that I must lead not only by words but by example.

***

My son, Aiden Christopher is my little hero. Though my days have seen some rough times, I draw my greatest strength from him. He gives me my reason for everything in life. Aiden, you have been my knight in shining armor, my hero, my salvation, and sometimes you have been my reminder to find humbleness. Thank you my love, for being the amazing young man you are day in and day out.

***

My friend, Steve, you were proud of me and believed in me when I was afraid. Thank you for pushing me and holding me accountable in ways that I needed.

***

My friend, Abeer, you have always been there and you were there to walk in when others seemed to have walked out. You taught me that true friendship can exist and that the world is still filled with good people, if you look for them.

***

Thank you to my readers, you, for making it possible for me to share my poetry with the world.

HIM

I take it
Absorbing each little word bullet
Breathe deep
Move forward

Waiting
Still
So long
So much
Waiting

My skin never thickens
My heart never hardens
My ears never grow depth
My mind never fails to comprehend
My soul never ignores it

Father
Dad
Daddy
Sperm donor
Child support payer
Trier of fatherhood
Nurturer of hate
Purveyor of anger

Poison
He tells me often that I am poison to him
Poison to his life
Poison to his happiness
Poison to what could have been easy

Should have been his way
Poison to his control of the situation
Poisoning what life could have been if he had never
Never married my mother
Never loved my mother
Never had a child

Evil
He tells me often that I am evil to him
I am the epitome of what hurts him
What makes his life difficult
What costs him money
Costs him time
A thorn in his side
In his way of living the life he wants and how he wants and who he wants
I cramp his style of hermitude

Hard to love
He tells me how hard it is
To love me
He barely can
No one probably ever really will
Love me

He's a predictor of the future
I'll get married, he tells me
I'll get divorced, he tells me
Then I'll know, he tells me
No one will ever be able to love me
He never lets me forget

It's my fault
Everything bad that has ever happened

To him, to the world, in his life
It's my fault
I do it
My mere existence
That's why he finally tells me
On the phone
When I live over 650 miles away
The words are said slowly
Deliberately

Why

Don't

You

Just

Go

*K I L L *

Yourself

Because

It

Would

Make

My

Whole

Life

A

Lot

Easier

Words so powerful
Words so purposeful
Words
Words
Words

Not just evil
Not just poison
Not just hateful
Murderous
If I let them be
Let them
No

Every single day
I push back against them

I try
Try
Try
Try

Love myself
Love those around me

Until someday
One day
Prove his words
Wrong
When I am
Loved

HOW MUCH

How much
Define it for me...please
How much is enough
How much is too much
I strive to be strong and struggle to survive
Stemming from a withered past how can I mend a wilting future
Take and give
Make and live
Beating heart and dripping tear
Forever paying for the shame
Created my own chains
It catches up with you
A thief in the night
Like a sword to the chest it takes your breath
Pay in every possible way
But don't forget to be thankful for what has not been lost...yet
Smile through tears and look up each year
Not day by day but rather moment by moment
They applaud the strength
Awe at the inspiration
Nothing comes free and so the toll must be paid
If all the sayings are true, promises of dreams made real...
I cannot wait for my
Tomorrow's ...tomorrow

PUSH, TRY

Pain knows no limit and respects no boundaries
Past, always haunting, never forgetting
Roots can never be denied
Can't escape what surrounds me
Trying, hard, harder, harder
HARDER
TRYING
Surrounds me, here, there...stop, stop stop
Can't breathe
Try try try try
Aren't you trying
??!!??
Just do it
Because you have to, no other choice
Do it
Just do it
Push
Push on, go forward
One foot, then other
Push push try try
Suck it up
Beautiful love growing every day
My will to live
Such a big purpose, such a little being
Must make it through
For him, I must survive
I give him life, he gives me life
This is the best, for now
What other choices do I have?
Why does the best have to be so bad?
So many choices, no allies, no comrades
Am I right

Am I wrong
Everyone questions, everyone doubts
I question, I doubt
No one sees
Do what is best, do what is right
What is best, what is right
Love so much, means so much
Can't mess up
Already messed up
Oops
Oh no
Trying trying
Try harder
Do better
Just have to
Not sure
Hoping
Praying
Wishing
Dreaming
Searching
Breathe
Love grows more and more
Stronger and stronger every day sprouting new leaves
So much love
So much pride
What do I do now
I am not sure
Heart bursting with love
Love overflowing
Love love love love
Trying pushing
Who am I?
Trying to find my way through the fog

Love remember love
Look at him, stay focused
Find a way, must find a way
Living in darkness, trying to create light
Can't see, can't feel
Being torn apart by savage lions
Painting the floating butterfly
Thirsty, searching, so thirsty
So much muck so much murk
Cloudy water never quenches thirst
Save love save self
Without any way
If only, if only
Mistakes, mistakes
Trading one misery for another
Push push
Try try
TRY
PUSH
Ugh!
Tired
Can't get tired
Go go go go go go go
Do this, do that…impossible?
No money
No education
Nothing
Love
My baby, I love him
For him
Push
Go
Do it
Try

Lost, gotta find…what am I looking for?
Feel good, going good
BAM
BAM
BAM
Cut, punch, scrape, bleed
Haha, they laugh
Brush it off
Turn cold, try, build a wall, try
Easy said, never done
Push, push push
PUSH TRY PUSH TRY
For him, give him something better
Save him from this
Save him
Push
Try
Push
Try
Push
Try
Push
Try
…

THEY ARE THE SUN

An undefined figure
No clear cut start or beginning
The roots unknown and blending into too many
Sometimes cut up in the most abrupt places
Places change, constantly moving
Walked on, stepped all over
Over looked by most, unseen by many
Bland and dull, always down and out
On the ground, the part ignored by the sun
No light to shine upon it, masking who defines it
A shadow, my shadow, am I
I got lost in my shadow, forgetting who and what I am
Easy to fade away, people hardly notice
Slink back and hide, ashamed and afraid
I lived in my shadow until I became that
That is until they would no longer stand for it
The sunlight of their love they cast upon me so brightly
Banish, banish, exile the shadow
The defenders of my destiny
Warriors against my worries and woes
My own gladiators for my gladness
Believing in me when I did not
Loving me when I forgot
They are the sun that refuses to allow
The shadows to claim me, define me or be me
They are the sunlight that makes me grow
Forcing me forward, the friends that frighten all foes

A REAL POEM

Many words have
seeped from my pen to
the world's paper.

On these petals of truth
much of my soul has been
spread between the lines.

I have forgotten all about
the core and laid before you
shell, skin and scales.

Giving it all bared naked
hiding as I could
I tried to give answers I didn't have.

Live from within out
let not law, rule nor stature
exile you from your passion.

A SPLINTERED SPELL

Brothers and sisters
They stand next to me crooked
Some straight, some broken
All crafted by the same hand
Standing like soldiers
Each other's only life source
Every role vital
Connected with unseen bond
One goal, one truth, one
Vision of a family
Memories to make
Just a picket fence to you
Masked beauty to me

GUILT

The moment is swiftly crawling.
Creeping, crouching, closer.
My heart beats in time with the clock.
Tick tock. Tick tock. Tick tock.
Beating.
Waiting.
Crying.
Anticipating.
Closer. Closer. Closer.
He rides on his dark horse through the night.
His breath on the back of my neck.
Hear the shrill pierce screams.
Fear breeding in the darkness of night.
Slowly. Swiftly.
Crawling. Around every corner.
Hell shivering in fright.
Revenge seeping from his yellow rotted teeth as ooze.
He breathes heavily.
Grunts as he rides along
The demon will not rest.
His icy cold heart is frozen with the desire of satisfaction.
Ridding. Ridding. Ridding.
Hard.
Harder.
Deliberately into the road.
Marking this moment.
Clunk…
Clunk…
Clunk…
Hooves of his mid-night horse pound the earth beneath.
The ground begs for mercy.

Dirt crumbles falling from depressing brown toned hair.
Freshly filled with life.
Blood courses through empty veins.
Breath seeps from tiny nostrils poisoning the air.
He's coming back.
Back to avenge his death…
with me.
His revenge.
My ankles shake with furry.
Knees succumb to the ground beckoning them.
Dragged down by chains of regret.
I look at the wooden boards below.
They rumble. They roar.
Hell has come to claim my soul.
Boney gray fingers reaching quickly for my throat.
As they near, I see the hand attached to my arm and body.
Closer until it has a death grip upon my neck.
Is it too late to say I'm sorry?

IN HIS HEART

Last words of I love you
Spilled from his quivering lips
Caught in a storm of pain
His body convulsing on the ground
The envelope of love he once existed in
Scattered among his lost memories
His crystal clear blue eyes
Falling back to forever rest
Unspoken vows searching in his soul
As a single salty tear is permitted to fall
The enemy has taken his youth, his heart and his freedom
All in one blow
His once supportive legs give way
His body crashed upon the earth
The lost love of happiness
Wanders lonely on the battlefield
A hung head
A target to Death
What hope could ever exist in the despair of the end
More drops of red
Red as a rose trickling down his body
Only to fall upon the black and white beauty
He so devotedly clutched in his hand
The image dancing in his mind
His beloved
With trembling hands he slowly brings her to his lips
A lover's last farewell
There she rests
For now
Forever
In his heart

MY sHAD*ow*

Unprepared.
Sure of WHAT is found untrue!!!
Trying every experience
DANcing amid risk
CAReless.
Free of security, stability, sound mind
imPERFECT so many ways
Unstable.
Sporadic spontaneous
Action. Reaction. Oops.
Dressed .
Bright VIBrant colors
DESTROYING shell of *sophistication*
Many times tears of turbulence TRICKLE
RoLlEr CoAsTeR rides of emotions
Land. Water. Air.
NEVER enough
Backing down an unknown gesture
A p i e c e
Everyone. Everything. Ambitious.
Choppy short straight hair
Trying everything you won't
short.
To the point living With attitude
MakIng a scene
Bright thickLy Lined eyes
POWER
Gaudy and tacky
Heavy lipstick. Heavier lip liner.
imPROPER
Speech slurred by laziness

Soaring.
Crashing.
Nothing unbelievable.
Trusting to be used.
Society's toy.
Too much. Too little.
Situations.
Relationship.
Time bombs waiting to go OFF
Shooting star
Breaking l o o s e !
Fighting a timeless war
Loss of pRIDE
Lacking affection
Losing worth
Biggest battle
Conquering self

REALIZATION

I used to try to figure everything
out, not being.

I could have understood it all in a
glance plain as day.

I wasted so much on what meant nothing,
and hindering

the beauty of what should have been and could
have been, still should.

I realize I must take time I got here
and hold it dear.

I'll do my best to see what's right in front
of me. No stunt

will stop me from grasping what I never
did. Whenever

the trivial presents itself I'll see
what it can be.

SEEING HIM

Through eyes of pain
Goggled with massive lenses of joy
Blinded by the darkness and pierced by the light
The storm dances in his very own soul
Looking deep questioning who has control
He whispers dreams in his sleep
Words seeping from his lips never to be spoken in daylight
Lowest of lows woe all woes for when the sunrises his dreams become improbable
Never good enough having no potential
I see him as he cannot see himself
Once the whole picture is revealed he will too see the beauty which hath been masked by his own hand

SELF ~~ESTEEM~~ TRUTH

I am
FAT.
It's no secret
why,
at least not
to me. I know, I remember
how it all
started. It was
on purpose. I got fat
on purpose and I stay
fat because it is all I know
how to do, or
all I deserve.
I'm still serving
time, a life
sentence.
I wallow
in
self pity; it is
the easiest
emotion for me
to feel. I get
"cheered up"
by being miserable;
it is
a healthy
reminder of how
I feel I should be
living my life. Sadness
is like a warm blanket
pity is the fire

that lights my way and
keeps me warm
on cold bitter nights.
I seek
hurt, when someone hurts
me I cling to them
tighter.
The pain they ration
out to me is like
food for my soul;
it feeds me
gives me strength
to trudge through
to the next day.
I am lonely
with few friends
when many are
a simple reach away.
It is better
this way, they would
make me happy
that would never do.
Does a star baseball player
who is now washed
up have a good time
watching the next big
shot in his place
doing it all better?
Does he miss
the fans
or the game
more?
What if
it's been so long

and he's so old
and crotchety
that the fans
don't even remember
liking him?
Some people cut
themselves
and watch the blood
flow out of them,
so soul soothing
such comfort and relief.
Trickle.
Trickle
Trickle.
Drip.
Drip.
Drip.
I do not
do that.
I wallow.
Try it.
Force
yourself to feel
every negative emotion
inside and out
upside down and right side
up.
Feel it.
Again.
Again.
Again.
Don't stop
and each little
teensy

weensy
negative thing,
let it open
the flood gates to the
roots of all your pain.
Embrace it.
Swim in it.
Feel it.
Again.
Again.
Again…
don’t ever stop!!!
Ah,
now
doesn’t that feel
so good,
so right,
so soothing,
so comforting?
That’s what is about
That’s what’s real
real, raw, real

THE BEDROOM I GREW UP IN

Sitting in the bedroom I grew up in…

Trickle, trickle, the tears always flowed abundantly in here

The pain and self pity almost always chocked the life out of me

Somehow within these four walls I survived my darkest days, my youth

I begged the Lord many a times for some understanding and clarity

"Why" would become the constant unsatisfied lust in my life

The white fuzzy worn Teddy whose age just about matched my own served as a girl's best friend

Alone in such a crowded life in which the liver creates constant chaos In search of cherished calm

The old days crawled by leaving behind it bottomless holes

My emotions, the wrecking ball shattering the fragile shell of my truth

Sitting in the bedroom I grew up in…

Are the memories painfully damaging or simply the sting of disinfectant on an open infected wound?

I spent my adolescence desperately trying to escape this room to find myself years later escaping to it

Who pens this, that, creating nothing and everything?

Will the past ever truly be buried when all the character walk through life with a shovel?

Although a book cannot be judged by its cover, do we not all walk around with our souls written on our faces?

A question for me is an answer for you a home and my home is your prison

Sitting in the bedroom I grew up in…

These walls have always been my bars; will they now be my ladders?

INESCAPABLE YOU

Poised in thoughtful contentment staring down air.
Sits in that little chair breaking subtle
waves endearment. Fear to rustle
common inadequate storage bears
one being into self-stored inner stares.
Battle fought within will not be muffled.
Conqueror will receive no rebuttal.
Can someone outside even care to care?
Quest of challenge will weigh and measure you.
Finding your true value will test your pride.
A victory is what will be found by few.
Hard to hide from the world harder to hid
from this new mirror encompassing you.
Buckle up and get ready for this ride.

NIGHTMARE FORCED TO LIVE

Memories haunt the pattern of my life
Shadows of laughter dance to a new tune
Forced to throw away the diamond
My mind runs in circles
The wool woven by my own hand blinds me
The fog is finally lifted
Friend blurs to foe
Surprises soft and sure begin to sting
Roses thrust their thorns
A rainbow missing color
The floods of found happiness drown me
Naïve to never predict
The shield turns to dagger
Life and earth become one and the same
What was once so dear taken
A fly caught with honey
Tasting the humbleness of vinegar
Silent stabs stir softly
Love only to be deceived

UNREACHABLE FOG

Misty cleansing of my soul
she helps unlock
the images hidden
even to myself
Creating a bubble
to lock the world
out and me in
Her laughter tickles
my cheeks and slowly draws up
the corners of my lips
She blankets my future
with smiles and warm cookies
around every corner
An enjoyable escape
giving me the power
to see only what I desire
Each inch of her
is full of vague emotions
belonging to the one who'll
unmask them,
unmask her

WHAT I FORGOT ABOUT THE WORLD

People tend to look away
When they catch each other in a stare.

Whenever you're in a rush to go somewhere
The traffic lights all turn red.

A strong leader preaches unification to his people
He allows another woman to sleep in his wife's bed

Hitler killed millions of families but
Valued his mother's life as sacred.

Kennedy, Lincoln, and Diana were killed in their prime.
Their potential hovering in the air of wonderment

If I had to choose between loving someone
Or having someone love me
I'd love them
Because to love someone else you must already love yourself

You long to find your inner true self
You buy books written by people
People who you never met

THE STORY OF A GARDEN

Friends and foes regularly weeded.
Completed with massive might.
Warm. Whispers. Tenderness. Unheeded.
Life for this bud out of sight.
Sun rise soon.
Will the dreariest of buds bloom?
This bud's destiny never comfortable.
From death could life be safe?
A miracle uncontrollable.
This place.
One bloom continued, hoped.
Her petal, kindest.
Failure never scoped.
Beauty timelessly mindless.
Bloom urged bud, hold on.
Strength for bud upon.
Passion. Vibrancy. Ignite.
No surprise.
Glory upon sight.
A new bloom, nothing to compromise.

EVERY FAMILY HAS ONE

Mistakes, everyone makes them but not necessarily to the magnitude of others. Why am I held to such a high standard? Why do I have to be so hard on myself? When you dig such a big hole reaching the surface may only be wishful thinking.

I am the Queen of Mistakes. You would have an easier time listing off the things I didn't do wrong than the things I did do wrong. I hurt a lot and not just me but often others.

I started at the top and fell to the bottom.

Others can hide all of their mistakes and troubles, God forgot to give me that talent.

Wanna know how I think or feel or need? Just check my sleeve. No hiding for me.

One step forward, oh so hard, so hard, so hard…one leap backward.

How do you define good? How do you find value in a person? What does happiness look like?

To be the fool smiling when everyone else is scowling or crying is punishable by the corner of shame.

Self-inflicted title.

Shaved every spring. Wool grows back same dark, deep , empty color.

THOUGHTS FLOATING THROUGH MY MIND…

For some reason, as I lie here in reflection of life lived, mistakes made and potential yet to be realized I have a collection of thoughts floating through my mind... So here they are, to share:

The silence heard when only in solitude is composed of the cries of all the truths the conscious you repeatedly, repeatedly, repeatedly refuses...

The pattern to which you design your life is the artwork of a soul hungry and thirsty for the passions bursting in your heart...

The drawing board of life is not a place to start over, re-create or re-design; but rather an opportunity to re-direct from a new perspective...

Excuses, omissions and lies are all just shame incognito.

The unrealized dream is born of fear.

Denial is the most addictive and abused drug.

Mistakes can either be scars or beauty marks, the choosing is yours.

Reflection is not a time of reminiscing or remorse, it is a time of creation and collaboration of the mind and heart.

Mistakes made over and over in cycles of life are not mistakes, but perhaps rather who and what you are choosing to be.

Self-control will always be a double-edged sword, denying desire to conform to unanimity but allowing the water to be stead, safe and sure.

Lessons unlearned are leashes unlatched on life.

THE SHADOW THAT RESIDES IN MY INNER MOST HEART OF HEARTS

Sometimes I wonder about the unknown, but mostly my thoughts are consumed by known things.

Why?

I want to truly understand all that is known to me.

I want to feel all that I feel deeper, make it more real.

How do I become more of who I already am?

The world intrigues me, and I have a hunger for its spirit.

Change consumes us inevitably and it thrills me.

More, because enough is never quite enough for me.

My thirst for living is unquenchable.

All possibilities and impossibilities, I must experience.

If I can think it, I can feel it...and if I can feel it, I can do it...and if I can do it, I can be it.

One more time is never my encore.

I always have more to say, another thing to do.

Hold me back and drag me away because God forgot to give me a filter.

Censorship holds no reins over me.

My will always seems to be the way.

The wake of my influence is felt farther and wider.

Adrenaline runs through my blood and no challenge I find goes unmet.

Look me in the eyes, I dare you.

Secrets unfathomable will seep from my skin if you get too close.

There will always be a page you have not read in my book.

Will you really allow me to out maneuver you?

Do not proceed if you can fear, because I will conquer you.

I am the woman they forgot to put the warning label on.

No warranty and no recall.

I am unreturnable because I will not cross your path and leave you untouched.

I am more and just a little bit less.

Confused yet?

You should be, the mess that makes perfect sense.

An organized chaos of a heart that struggles even to unravel itself.

I am who I am and I make no apologies.

My gut generates true power over my destiny.

I know no boundaries, as life is my greatest experiment.

The toys of my world consist of the pen in my hand the paper to which it makes beautiful love.

And if my love is something you think you can stomach, then I will meet you in the ring.

Be ready to fight, unless you fall too fast and give me the freedom to fly.

I will take you into my world and together we will redefine all that believes it has been defined.

Ready?

Alright, then let's get ready and you get ready because this you will never forgot.

You will never forget, it just is not possible!

Not unless...

Not unless...

Unless you are me, and then forgetting is just the lie you tell yourself to get to sleep at night.

...when you can sleep.

CONFESSION OF THOUGHTS

The days pass and moments move

A breath, a step, life goes forward

The heart such drive a rival of the mind

Mind and heart confused in a chaotic harmony with such competitive contempt

Enter into the forest and face every imaginable challenge

Survive and you will be a true treasure to behold

Get lost forever and forgotten you shall become

Fate, fear, future, fucked…fastened into freedom

Rolling through the mind excuses and lies to rest at night

Self

Versus self

Versus selfish

Unselfishness

A bleeding heart may save neighbor souls but the host can never survive

The levels of loneliness are limitless

A void to be filled, a hole left gaping

What shall they receive when all the giver has to give is gone

Who will applaud or appreciate the last man standing

What is the right in doing what is right when the truth is always clouded and grey

A perspective, a vision only ever shared by one

Is it beautiful or foolish to believe in something better

The ideas and the creativity without the opportunity or tools

A hunger so deep and passionate never to be fulfilled

The greener grass always lies in someone else's pastures

And wisdom always comes a second too late

To be honest and true, open and real, a heart on the sleeve

Such desirable ways, a way of life to only be taken for granted, abused and used

Victory for the vulnerable is unheard of for reasonable reasons

I swear from lips only genuine words flow

My eyes tell you the stories that my heart wishes to forget

The smile painted, sewn or bursting will be there nevertheless

A new day, but true to self never a new way

Of course, I shall always be okay, I have to be

For you see, if I am not, who else will be there when you need me

TRUTH

The hardest mistake to face
The reflection of thy self
True to be true to see
What about what cannot be seen
Does this physical shell protect or betray
A trick, a lie, a joke
Are you entertained yet
Have you had your fair share yet
Down the hatch and into the soul
The good the bad and plenty more
Experiences of making and breaking and taking
Born to be a fighter, a lover, a mother, a sinner, a believer, a creator
Trial after trial and test after test
The results measure the same
Blame and misery can only be passed for so long
The circle always brings them home
The wails of wicked truth can make a person go deaf
Time after time one cannot help but wonder
How can it not be me
How can I not see
What foolish things I have believed
But now I know not how to be redeemed
For within my life I have lost the esteem
And perhaps even my ability to dream

CANNOT LEARN

What happens when you cannot learn
You teach and you share and you gain knowledge
You know facts and understand concepts
But your heart overpowers your mind
Your fears somehow always disappear, at the worst of times
Learned lesson unlearned so easily, not really learned at all
Yet, the mistakes continue to be made
Same, same, same, same
Fall
Fall fast
Fall hard
Fall and forget
Fall banish fears
Fall
Down, down, down you go
The heart cannot grow calluses
The heart charges forward as if it never felt pain
But the pain comes
Eventually
The pain always comes
You know, you're aware, you get it, you understand
In the midst you can even see it coming, sense it
Surprise still washes over you, like a stupidity
Yet…somehow…you cannot change your ways
You cannot learn, intelligence, intuition have no value here
You just cannot,
ever...ever...ever...ever...ever...ever...ever...ever...
Seem to learn, not ever

BE HAPPY

How might our happiness be defined
Each individual a unique belief
Happiness
Being happy
Feeling…well, happy
Living, hmm…mmm…yes, happily
What defines happiness
Might it be the heart
The mind may take control
Perspective has such control over much
Perhaps attitude
No
The answer is just not clear
Could sadness possibly outline the definition of happiness
Is there space between the two
Do they blend together and might life hover back and forth between boundaries
Is my happiness your sorrow and my sorrow your happiness
What kind of life could that possibly promise tomorrow
Truth, we can each have our own
View, something often skewed and greatly influenced
Interpretation, limitless to possibilities and manipulation
So then, if one wishes to be happy and does not know who or what that might be
Well, then what
Happy or sad, sad or happy
Might this be ignorance, disability, stupidity
Maybe, what it is -----whether conscious or not
Self-sabotage
So what is happiness

How do you define and better yet…
How do you decide if you even deserve it

I KNOW…I KNOW…I KNOW

The balance of love and reality is so unreal
Love is beautifully deceiving and yet so damn relieving
How can the cure all be so damaging
Nothing for free, everything a cost
Can't give what you don't have
Can't see what you choose not to
Conditionally unconditional
The truth no one wishes to admit
The reality is my truth
Pleasant it is not always
Promised to live without regret
…regretting that promise
Inspiringly painful the woulda coulda shouldas haunt my mind
Do it different
Be a little different
Try again
Can't, too late…just too late
It wasn't a lapse of memory
It was a lapse of self-control
What does it take
What suffering must be made
Are scars not enough
Death of desire does not damage enough
You know, you understand, you even agree
Why can't you then be
Determined so much to prove harsh words wrong
That focus is lost and gone
Prove wrong fast and sure, so much so that…
The opportunity goes away…quick, quick, quick
All that's left then is the drip, drip, drip

A bleeding heart is good company for no one
A broken heart demands patience and craft
A hollow heart grows cold and bitter in no time at all
But the strongest of hearts beats on and goes again
Even if the cycle repeats because you cannot learn if you do not do
So do, and be, and don't give up on trying to truly see

THOUGHTS OF THE MORNING

If life is short and we know not what comes our way
tomorrow…
Why do we waste such time wallowing in worries and
sorrow?
Happiness in contagious yet why is it so rarely found these
days?
What is taught and preached…
Rules and boundaries so often breached.
To aspire and to dream, beautifully
To be and do, too unsuccessfully.
Today I woke up, half-awake still dreaming
I wondered about events that passed
Dreams and reality blend together,
What is reality and what is desire…could a little fear be
mixed in
Maybe the bridge I've crossed is one of
Enjoying reality better than the dreams of my sleep
It all seems so much more possible
Hope is best received when you give it to yourself
A dream is achieved only when your heart really wants it
The dimensions of reality are only limited by the
Fear you allow to enter into your mind
What defines goodness and purity is determined by self-
perception
Beauty is in the eye of the beholder,
Choose carefully who beholds you...
And be cautious about those you choose to behold.

UNTITLED

Soft and subtle wind dancing with the autumn leaves of my life
Whispers from my conscious lips speak of unfound truth somewhere down the road

Using dreams, escaping from the world with which I feel imprisoned

His lies shoot through my heart like unwritten torture as he kills the most trust I so devotedly had in him

The smooth sound of her enchanting voice coating over the sorrowfulness of her audience that today has aguishly ceased

INHALE. EXHALE.

Inhale. Exhale.
In. Out. In. Out.
Breathe. Keep breathing.
Ding. Dong. Doorbell.
Anticipat-
ing hand, fingers
crawl around knob
Turn and open.

It's sort of odd
each set of eyes
sees differently.
Tells another
story. Speaks hid-
den truths. All sub-
consciously per-
forming the same
task. What is u-
nique about his?

Moments
fill with desi-
re, but masked with
silence. Doesn't
he see deep in-
to me? Can he
hear the thoughts I'm
too afraid to
reveal from with
inside myself?

Wrinkles crease all
hands. An unmatch-
able pattern.
Every line weaves
a different
wear and tear. Ex-
perience draw-
ing traces of
wisdom. Fingers
branch out for in-
dividual-
ism. But root
all from same hand.
Carrying same
prints and lines.
What does his read?

From afar the
eyes seem to blend.
One solid u-
unique shade from
the rainbow. A clos-
er look reveals
a deeper beau-
ty. Intricate
lines weave a web.
Quite a sticky
tricky one that
I've seemed to be-
come entangled
with no hurry
to free myself.
Will he let me
make it my very

own home sweet home?

Shoot tingles
fingertip to wrist. Heated
cheeks blend pink with
anticipa-
tion. Connected
palm to palm.
Lines and creases
blend creating
new beginning.

Closer. Closer.
Inch by inch we
almost connect.
Give me a sign,
please any sign.
Does he feel what
I am encom-
passed with? If he
only would...just...
do...that...just that!

One night down. For-
ever more to
go. Thump, thump, thump.
Calm heart. Calm down.
Collapse on bed.
Breathe. Keep breathing.
In. Out. In. Out.
Inhale. Exhale.

LAUGHTER

Laughter echoes the hallways of my memory today,
Derek playing his prominent trumpet,
The notes of his organ perpetuating through the air,
Three best friends swore their bond would last through to the end,
Jack running and reaching his athletic goals,
Re-tracing the steps of the men in his family,
Common blood flows through their veins,
Renee leads the group loving the role,
Her life mistakes become the lessons for all three to learn,
Each individual identifies themselves with idealistic talents,
The boys confess they once dressed in curls,
That girl could not stand a boy having the upper hand,
Concerts and plays at every family event,
Until one day that bond reached a place of no return,
A tear...a snap...a break...a yell...a slap...a no more...
What was once so much now is nothing,
Derek moved away placing dedication at a distance,
Jack chose a bumpy road sacrificing character,
Renee wanders lost in dramatic emotions,
Laughter echoes the hallways of my memory today,
Yesterday laughter echoed the hallways of my heart.

DIRECTION

Alone we travel this road together
Sometimes unable to decipher direction
Life's surroundings drown out all consciousness
You move in the pattern of repetition, and routine
Forward
Backward

Turning not an option
Forced of fate find you fiercely direction
Traveling a t a never-ending increasing speed
Time is racing for a victory to share
Left
Right

As long as you're traveling no destination is required
Existence on this path, all you know
Nothing is odd because everything is strange
Yesterday forgotten and tomorrow unknown
Up
Down

Blindly led no wrong turns are chosen, no mistakes are made
This road leads to the same destination

me

so FUNny
i + mirror = I
i i i i diminish
POPular
deFLATes
I shine
BRIGHT
B
BEautiful
ING me
MElting shell
getting to
K
N
O
W
who I am?
STOP!
the in inside
capitalized
IN me
me
me
MEdia
tries to alter
but ME remains prominent
...
!!!HEY!!!
me, ME

MUSIC

Notes written on a line
Words dancing in my mind
Feelings you cannot describe

Can't tell you
Can't show you

Music will give you sight
Let it guide you, be your light

Music will give you sound
Go ahead and scream out loud

Open your soul and let it dance
Let go, give it freedom to take control
Release your mind to get a chance

Music will give you sight
Let it guide you, be your light

Music will give you sound
Go ahead and scream out loud

Your body pulls to the rhythm and beat
Flowing over you with such intense heat

You'll crave it in your bones
Let it feed your hunger
It will be your only home

TO WRITE

The pen touches the paper gracefully staining it indefinitely with ink. Each movement controlled
and carefully calibrated by the fingers. One touch, every touch is forever never to be erased nor forgotten. Long and slender they encompass the pen's long and slender goose neck like body. Strokes sometimes fast and others slow empowering the pen with language.

The hand and pen united as if one move left to right similar to the pendulum in an old grandfather clock. Hand, fingers and pen slide along the paper, so soft and so smooth reaching the end to take a long refreshing slide back to the left side, back to the beginning.

Head bent, craned low, a tiger patiently waiting to pounce on its prey. Admiring, lusting eyes seem to have a fire brewing inside as they examine the work of each stroke the pen takes. History is being created leaving something forever.

Brows furred in intense thought. Strand by single strand, hair falls forward inching closer and closer to its longing.

Words dance across the paper that once was so blank and empty. Meaning and purpose with language seek out from the sheets, a sponge thirsting for more.

A deep breath of inspiration is taken as the writer eases back in the chair. Back is arched and hands reach upwards toward heaven. A stretch of satisfaction, but only so far. Deeply sighing the writer knows work is not finished. The once again find its home.

Finger by finger the pen is enwrapped in its destiny. Just enough ink in its purposeful body to finish its single and most important task. The body a gun and its ink the bullets killing all obstacles in its execution.

Up and down, left and right, no matter which direction the pen flows it's a right one. Guided by the seemingly wise hand the pen acts as servant to its master.

Skin tightened around knuckles where any grasp is tight and secure. Fine lines seen only by the curious eye crease the hand. Time and wisdom have left both of their marks. Nails bitten and gnawed with frustration over years of writers block and fallen dreams. Everything only to inspire the task now at hand.

Every daily task overlooked by an ordinary eye creates inspiration and food for thought. Actions, thoughts, observations all used to fuel the pen still dancing along the paper. Lines horizontal across the paper fill the sheet with hunger hurries to the next sheet almost forgetting to breathe.

The pen writes no more, movements already acted upon. Ink has dispersed and all that is left is the masterpiece and memories filled on the sheets surrounding the writer. Their environment is their life.

RAMBLINGS OF A CLOUDY DAY

The sun is there every day
When I can see it and even still when my eyes are clouded
It is there screaming and streaming
The message heard is that with which I choose to hear
But remember, we all must, that the day is never over until it is over
And that tomorrow the sun will rise again
If all I have is this moment, this cherished moment
Cherish it I will and to you I wish
The patience I struggle to grasp
The moments of past I let go
The smiles I forgot to wear
The risks I feared to take
And the second chances I never got
Some wisdom cannot be gained after the first mistake
Just as some lessons are not learned from others but only
From the paths we tread ourselves
Nothing worth having comes without struggle
For which you feel fulfilled and true
It is earned, for we all have dues we must pay
There can be beauty even in damage
And though broken to one a project to another
There is always a right fit, a genuinely true way
And while the tide can be a blessing or a curse
What it all comes down to is to what it all is worth
So I sit here contemplating, but truly the answer I know not
For the revelation will come only from you
I'm alright, and I'll be just fine…for tomorrow dear
I believe will be divine

THE FLUFF AND WHITE

The fluff and white

Coverings of a beauteous dream
The dream to be torturously
Within reach to awake
Steps thought forward, backward still
A hope given flight
To be gone from grasp
The wonder withheld
Until the wind blew
Cold and bitter

The fluff and white

Away, blown to the side
A ray to break through
Two more to follow until
The warmth engulfs
The life restored
So this is what it is
What it is supposed to be
The travels and trials
Toward this triumph
I weathered through the many storms
Of my life and perhaps
Just perhaps, I may believe
My reward is just beginning

Goodbye fluff and white

No more will I be fooled
Taunt some other

For the sun has shone upon me
And I have finally tasted
And I finally know
I feel it, warm and fuzzy
Growing stronger inside

Despite the fluff and white

TO BREATHE…

To breathe…
So simple, so pure
It is within my grasp
To remedy life's foolish cure
The roads I've traveled
A plethora of torture, triumph
Dripping with the pleasure of others
The cost of me mangled
I walk this path, chosen
To keep the peace, merely appease
The cost of freedom, only to have risen
Shackled by the happiness of others
I must finally demand release
And thus I go
To breathe…
So simple, so pure

MAGNET

The magnet within my cavity pulls
To resist would be fatal
To let go makes me so fragile
The melody within in me to fuse
With the rhythm of another
I must dive in
To sink or to swim
My fate in their palm
Truth lies in fact
No choice is here to be made
The reality stands as is
I am here, my roots already planted
Forward I move
No more pulls, for the source
Has already been gifted
Perhaps even without my knowing
But the days have shown
Beauty and happiness like
None I have ever known
Tomorrow unknown, it matters not
For in this moment, from this moment
I know

TRUTH IN THE FOG

I walk in a world unsure
The shadow that consumes my past
Will often haunt my future
Figure not quite defined
Between the lines so hard to read
The message clear as day
Though my mind cannot comprehend
Perhaps it is because the heart muddles it all
What seems so defined and true today
May be torn to shreds tomorrow
To trust, trust the moment of now
Tomorrow holds fears turned to reality
I know not what to believe
The feeling, the moment, the now
The possibility, the failure to the reality
Dreams are so much easier
Ignorance provides sought bliss
To walk in the shadow of what might have been
A miserable torture, preventable
Backwards, forwards, around we all turn
Direction and focus never quite earned
Who we are and what we might be
The possibility potentials poisonous
Fatal to stand still
Requirement of being
To take moment, to stop breathe
It will make now harder
Tomorrow better
And future, maybe possible
Is it plausible to risk it all for possible
How much self-inflicted questions

Unanswered truths
You ask for it, and you shall receive
But whether you want
Truth and Trust
Can you stomach it?
Will it destroy you?

WE BE

What is what we are
Who are we
Be
The essence of events
We walk, we tread
Forward to move
I go, I live, I survive
No other option
Skin tough, yet heart still so weak
To penetrate is to break
Fragile and deadly
One shot, one blow, one chance
All or nothing
Nothing or all
Do it or don't
Never in between
The world has no niche for me
So the world I must change
Define me, label me…I am not
Able to be categorized
I am me
You are you
We are who we are
We just be

USED TO BE, AM

I used to be…
So many things change
Sometimes for better
Sometimes for worse
I used to be this person…
I loved her and hated her
She was my all and yet my demise
Her strengths so damn strong
Her weaknesses fucking weak
All or Nothing
Everything and Somethings
Trying is never good enough
A shadow cast within
The darkest bright you've ever seen
On fire and alive
The best of the best
Worst of the worst
No package perfect
The epitome of irony
I used to be, who I am
Or am I now becoming who I used to be
I don't know
But one thing is certain
Whether I used to be or I am
My flavor is ever changing
But never for the worse
Always for the better
I am an artist not satisfied with my
MASTERPIECE
It is a treasure, and of it I am proud
My name I sign with pride

But perfection is a goal I
Will always seek
I used to be, I am
Used
Am
I
Yes
I am because I used to be
Therefore
I used to be I am

f_e_a_r

Fears
Unavoidable, but completely able to be DESTROYED
The power possessed only the power given
Excuses for our failures
Vehicles which we hide behind
Rise to the challenge
Or cower in your own shadow
We are who we choose to be
Authors of our own definitions
Designers of our destiny
Let fear dictate
Or dictate your fear
A wild savage
Tamed with the right attitude
Will power must be wanted and not wanting
Fear, forevermore
The bare bones of our being
Be it friend or foe
Fear is there, it is here
Lining the most wondrous of treasures
Are you thirsty for life, for destruction of fear
I have an unquenchable thirst to live

UNLEASHED

I wait in silence
For the noise to return to me
The comfort of chaos
Chastisement in creativity
Willing to be me in all shades
Arise once more
Enter into the depths of it all
Unite and become the oneness of design
Forge something unbreakable between
Release

RAIN IN MY HEART

The rain in my heart comes and goes
Down pour heavy when it flows
Storm accompanied by a fog of confusion
To penetrate the clouds the sun must be
Strong
Sure
Safe
Secure
Sometimes the storm will pass with ease
Other, a flood is sure to come
But pass, I know, the storm eventually does
The wind that suddenly blows away the bitter dampness
Comes in many forms
Many faces it wears
It's origin not always known
Cycles of life never-ending
The pattern of weather unpredictable
A frozen moment last not a mere second
Measuring life in minutes, moments, meaning
A breath too sudden or hesitant
May just be the difference
That makes all the difference
Drip, drop
The rain in my heart

LOVE

Love
Definition limitless
Feeling, indescribable
Restraint and label, bound for failure
Love
Beauteous, contagious
Irrepressible, despite effort
Baggage or fear holds no true power
Love
It will conquer every battle
Stronger than you think
Truer than you can imagine
Love
A whisper that SCREAMS
Ignorance will not be your bliss
Pretend, lie…there it be
Love
See it, know it, believe it
Or not, for it matters not
Growth, unending and not preventable
Love
Run if you must
But follow it will
Haunting your dreams and lining your what ifs
Love
There she be
Love

ALL THAT REMAINS

Years come and go
Kind they have been not
Wisdom comes
The cost high, bearing freedom
Not free, never free
Worth having, worth earning
Fighting
Being
Learning
Easy is lazy and lazy brings no hopes or joys
Shaped and refined
The diamond from coal
Under the hottest of fires
Comes the most beautiful stone
Swallowing pride
Leaping in blind
For at the end of it all
The fears, tears and dears of our days
Are all that remains

...transItion

An aide and way to pass
From one to the next
Transition
She guides you, grows you and gives to you
A moment to settle
Until the next best thing
Pass the time
To later pass her by
An open heart is often seen
As an easy heart
To clean you up
A band-aide, nothing more
But does the job
For now
Maybe even tomorrow
But nothing in life is ever permanent
Transition
Conveniently, clean and quick
Painlessly painful only for her
Task done, hard part through
Transition
Use her, abuse her and then
Finally lose her

WITHIN, KNOW…

tIny flutter of a dream

breath to barely tickle your lips

mist of fog escAping to blend into surrounded air

just a touch dancing far and More than wide

see you cannot, touch not to be

contagIous to the most of ambition

swirling from here to there and Nowhere

powered by hopeS

possible Possibilities

the faIth of one fertilizing

inside sometimes ratheR known by

onE to some people

irritateD by that of others

really truly only! fear holds the gates

dare to be materialized!

IN YOU, ME

Moments pass and fade from within our grasp
Close to being me, but often parts forgotten
Self-criticism projected from within that of others
To please, to appease, to conform

Then tomorrow's possibilities
Stained on my heart to become promises
And within myself I felt it grow strong, potential

Fear surrounded me and I masked it with strength
Further and further from myself I grew
Fooling even myself that I was being true

Then I found myself and I, reunited
Truer, deeper and more me I returned
The passions of my soul reignited

I walk now, with stronger purpose
A firm deliberate step
And to my side…
There you tread today and tomorrow's
World with me
And there are moments I find myself
In you, there, here

TO DECIDE

I know, not having to be told
The whispers of experience fall on my ears
The eyes, they have stories to tell
I don't just hear, I listen
I don't just observe, I see
Truth has been my friend and foe
Insight
An old soul
Today better than tomorrow
Now
This moment
What good is a gift you cannot
Use to better the self
I stumble
But fall...
Never
Not yesterday
Not today
And definitely not tomorrow
Before it passes
Will my destiny fade
Can it slip between my fingers

CHOICES

Trading one sorrow for another
Weighing and measuring
The dilemma of having a choice
Voice we know not how to use
A childish way of life
Knowing and understanding
Just not able to be doing
Everyone's problems are biggest to them
Every hurdle is the hardest we've faced
Every excuse tied to guilt
Bargaining
Such good convincers
We make choices
We make sacrifices
Justifications for mistakes as we make them
To pretend
No...
To lie to ourselves
That we have it all
The facade
Is it for the world
Or for you
Is it...
For me

BENEATH IT ALL

The scars I bare

Create my definition

And the smile I wear

Has traveled a journey you know nothing of

My strength was earned

Tests I've met

Challenges I've found

Opportunities sought

And sacrifices I've made

What you don't know

Maybe you cannot understand

ONE

I am the one...
They come to me for answers
A shoulder always available
Outstretched hand strong enough to grasp yours
I will support you
I will carry you
I will make up for your shortcomings
I am the one...
Compassion flows from me freely
I am the mirror that shows
Truth unable to be faced
Beauty cast aside
Masked emotions guarded against others
All know, asking is not even necessary
I am the one...
Who is the pillar
But what happens when the pillar
Needs repair, or reinforcement
A remodel or something more
What happens when the one...needs...some other one

I DON'T KNOW

Pause
Just hold on
Only temporary
Time out
Love not lost
All the same
Perhaps completely different
Soon...one day
Be patient
It's still there
Not stunted growth
Hibernation
Survival of the fittest
Time will pass
Nothing is permanent

...

Wait

...

Wait

...

Does
That
Mean

…

Is it fading?
Is it forgotten?
Is it forever?
Unanswered questions
Breed

MISSconception

MISSunderstanding

MISSing

It all

MY TIME

We miss the care
No longer helping the neighbor
Smiling at the stranger no more
Too closed off
Too closed-minded
Yet, we complain
Taught to thrive on
Fear
Protecting everything
All so fragile that
We're so careless
A disposable mindset
Recycling bad old habits
Of walking backward
With an illusion of progress
Closer and closer and closer
To getting further and farther
Away
From truth
From beauty
But mostly
From
One another

THE SEED

Our thoughts and feelings only
Have the value that we give them
An idea can only be made a plan
If at first we entertain it
Develop it, nurture it to grow
That is how the moment can turn into
The next
And the next
Better to think
"At least I know now..."
Than to wonder
"What if..."
What if?

STORY OF A COFFEE SHOP

The chit-chat of the crowd around me

Subdues into a soundtrack of inspiration

I have not been here, visited this

Inner part where my mind and heart connect

In too many moons

Suddenly my pen is gliding cross the white sheets before me

I find solitude in the crowd

Music barely peeks through the many voices surrounding me

Soft, to set the mellow mood

Exchanges of flirtation...a first date

Gossip between giggling young girls

Wives meeting to complain about their husbands

A group of old friends...no time seems to have passed between their busy lives

Hugs and high fives

Laughter and longing looks

The couple...could it be the start of lust or love

The girls...how their conversation will change in just a few years

The wives...will they go home happily appreciating their own husbands

The friends...will they be here again to catch up in another decade

I see them all as intervals of a whole life

Together they tell a story, but who will be there to

Write it, read it and celebrate it

Highlights of their conversation rattle through my mind and I ponder how it is I see them

All to make my thoughts wander some more

Just how they might see me

What part of the story am I

IGNORANCE

At which point
What and when and why
Did ignorance go from being
A curse to a choice
Was it ever just one or the other
At a time when ignorance can no longer
Be the excuse
And yet it still exists
So the question must be asked
Has ignorance gone from curse to choice to curse to what
Or was the curse of ignorance lined with
Happy relief of
Not having to think
Or question
Or know
Or care
Being able to look the other way
Pretending not to see
Forgetting the unpleasantries
And denying responsibility
So I ask you
What will you choose
Will you be ignorant
And turn the once curse from yourself
Into the curse you give the world

UNKNOWN

Thoughts of yours are questions

Anticipations of your moves

Motives of your heart

Rattle inside me like mysteries without a detective

Unanswered questions and unspoken expectations

Can become

Harmful

THE TRUTH IS…

The truth is you don't know me
Nobody knows me
Sometimes I forget myself
But then I'll take a moment to pause and remember
The truth is the truth isn't always clear
While tomorrow may be hazy
Today may be even more unclear
The truth is you don't know always know
And sometimes I don't always know
But somehow I get there
And usually I'll take you there too
The truth is nobody knows me
You don't know me
There's so much that I hide
Mostly it's the pain inside
But I find a way to survive
And tomorrow comes whether I want it to or not
And every morning I must wake up and face the day
Despite any dismay
And somehow I find the smile
I have to put on my face
To go on about, and do what I must
For there are those that love me
Depend on me and need me
And the truth is...
Well the truth is, I need them too

BECAUSE I DO

I'm not as together as I seem
And sometimes I need help
Though you'll never find me asking
Pride is not what hinders
More the notion to be strong
I am the survivor
And I've learned to survive on my own
So to have to need another
A weakness
A road I've traveled before
To learn from mistakes
An addict to play with temptation
So you ask me how I am
You wonder how I do it
Answers I cannot give
Because all I know is I go forward
Forward I go because
Well
I know
I just have to
Because I do

WHEN?

Sometimes, most of the time, always

There's a bigger picture
Your moment may overshadow yours
But in mine it's not the whole

Sometimes, most of the time, always

It isn't going to be fair
No uniform definition
Shades of gray and uncertainty

Sometimes, most of the time, always

It's the hard and trying times that
Make and shape and create you
Easy times are most often forgotten though captured
In heart and photo

Sometimes, most of the time, always

A mask is worn not to hide
But to shield
The difference being composed of pride and weakness

Sometimes, most of the time, always

It is the silence which holds the power
Over the loudest voice
The lack of action greater in presence
Than the grandiose gesture

Sometimes, most of the time, always

We see what we wish
Hear only what's desired
And excuse what we refuse to know

Sometimes, most of the time, always

What's done is done
Because the moment will pass
And now is sometimes, most of the time...

...

...

Always

MORE

when the shades of gray
of the day
have taken their toll
sometimes I forget
all that was meant in
the forging of my soul
the dream unwieldy as
is really just
the heart shielded
time to write my own happy ending
finished complaining
beginning creating
sustaining and behaving
forget negotiating
'cause there's more
than there seems
even to myself
in my mind I tell lines
masking the cries of a
truth untold
an ignorance is such bliss
compared to lost in the abyss
from the world's purity sold
beauty in the eye of the beholder
is really giving each its
own controller
time to write my own happy ending
finished complaining
beginning creating
sustaining and behaving
forget negotiating
bursting from deep within the corners of my soul

there years something so much more than you'll ever know
every understand, ever truly believe
'cause there's more
than there seems
even to myself
yes there's more
I'm so much more
than there seems
if only I could make the whole world see
I'm more than I seem
'cause I'm more
than I seem
perhaps, just maybe
even to myself

WE TRY

Opportunities that

are oh so fathomable

remain in a state of being

intangible

Possibilities of potential

possessing a power that

prowls perplexing to ponder

a poisoned perception

only the plight of the present

Yet still...

Somehow, someway

We try

AS I BE

I write as I feel
I feel as I breathe
I breathe as I am
I am as I am as I be
For bound by the chains of this destiny
I set in stone my pace and way of face
Defining as I discover and create
Naming only to categorize label and logic
Interpretation for the fool and expression for the muse
Retouch to reconnect with myself
Mindless ways of must and lust
Tragedy of beauty and joy of wretchedness
A choice, a way, a voice
This I write to be right
In the way I am
I am as I am as I be
See, now you see me

WHERE AND WHY?

Where are you?
Why have you abandoned me?
Your back is turned
Have I not gone through enough?
I know I have the strength
Thus far I've had the endurance
But I'm losing steam
Getting tired
I can't do this anymore
And yet you do nothing
Why do those who suffer continue in pain and those of fortune bask in their fortune?
Did you choose me to walk this path or has my good intentions led me to be a fool?
I've been faithful and true
God, where are you?
I ask you, plead, and beg
Help me Lord, please
Hold me up for I know how much longer
I can stand

I CAN BECAUSE I AM

I can because I am
You look at me and see
Nothing but smooth waters
Little do you recognize
The calm that proceeds and follows
A mighty massive storm
Is all that you witness
I am strong, strength I have
Much unknown or unrealized
I have survived
Withered and weathered
Strong, standing firmly
But what I lack the most
Be the endurance I covet
Trained my heart
Trained the soul
Found a smile in the darkest of darks
But suddenly I see
A discovery of weakening
A hand to hold
Shoulder to cry
Arms to catch
Push to move
I'm ready
To take my turn
Ready to be the one
Asking
Maybe

EXISTENCE I SEE OF ME

When the shades of gray from the day
Remain
Ponders of wonder rattle in a battle
Contained
Probability of possibility caught within a storm
Refraining
From expression beyond repression internal
Pains
A chaotic soul deprived of being revived
Sustained
Merely upon a breath of hope in attempt to cope
Refrains
Exist as magnet to stagnant too weak
Mainly
Infliction came by and to one and same

WHISPER OF HOPE

Kindness has strayed from simplicity
Somewhere lost it remains between intention and motive
Definitions and clarity have all evolved into the sculptor's clay
Friend or foe, foreboding or faithful
The image reflects distortion to a point of void
The fool now trusts as the wise man lusts
Backward world, inside out and ragged worn
Rebuilt from the ashes of waste
Credence and cheers for veneer and generic
Diving deep into shallow waters
Tread, nay float upon the labor of misfortunes
To this desire, deemed a dream
Embrace empathy, implore you I must
Strive, do not succumb to this hindrance
Rise above and shatter the facade
Invoke a new dream for this world
Awaken us from this taunting trance

DREAMS

Only taste of love
Contained within moments of dreams
Traveling parallel
To world
At times a cavity

A touch
A whisper
Feel two soft lips
Grace my own

Craving
Just a bit more
A moment longer
Eyes shut
Dreams desired
Desperate for dreams
Embracing any encore

To feel
My hand within
Another

Awaken the dead
Revive my heart

Shadows of love
All this heart
Permitted

Mere crumbs to sustain
Hungry heart

Enduring
Expectations shrouded in defeat
Escaping

Only dreams
Take me from one
Day to another

ACCEPTANCE

A ditch dug deep exists between
Acceptance and Tolerance
Ignorance incognito as Naivety and Laziness
The power in owning oneself
Owning truth
Accepting those for as they are
A challenge I set to you
Change the World
Only start within instead of ending up without

YOUR MASTERPIECE

There is something to be said
about what's left lingering
unspoken words never to be heard
a touch that's never shared
unexpressed emotions

As artists we aim to sculpt our lives

The presence of the present ignored is an artist without his medium
This moment, this now, is your masterpiece awaiting its creation

FOR YOU, MY FRIEND

We seek advice when the path is crystal clear

Hope drives doubt
Denial hinders humble acceptance
Lying to self feeds the flame of the facade

Losing one's way is plainly and purely that
No dressing up in designer self-sacrifice
No loss of self incognito as compassion
Changes the truth

Live by the heart
Live by the mind
Live by the moment

In the end we remain firm
In that the choices we make shape who and where we are

Happiness is a choice you make
Over and over
Purpose is a choice you make
Over and over
Self-worth is a choice you make
Over and over
Love is a choice you make
Over and over

As you make these choices each day in your life
I will serve as your mirror, your truest friend, your reminder
Of who and what you are

Until your authentic and best self stands before me
Your forced reflection I will be
Making you see just who the world now sees

KNOW

It's not something for which I should hold you accountable

I don't expect you to know, and definitely not to understand
I have not shared, and my story isn't one to just sit and tell
I can't even know where to begin

There are things I can tell you,
some that must be shown,
others to be shared by those around me,
some for you to learn for yourself.

To truly appreciate what is before you,
it is important to comprehend,
the journey it took to get there,
and to become what you see before you..

The perspective with which you conclude will be one of your own.

Deep:
as a thinker
as a feeler
as a lover
as a believer
Deep.

The depth has been dug by the journey undergone:
by choice
by consequence,
by circumstance

Should the path shared be fleeting or forever
Lives will have touched and shaped one another

HEAR TO LEARN

I have known more than a few days when the knowledge of where my head would rest at night was unknown.
I have celebrated.

I have broken.

I have survived

In my care has been a loved one journeying through their last days.

I have been used.

I have been abused.

I have been admired.

Beaten I have been by words and fists belonging to those adorned by my love.

I have been the glue.

I have been the knife.

I have been the sponge.

Battles I have fought of self-loathing and aimless self-pity.

I have failed.

I have succeeded.

I have tried.

Stolen from me more than just material goods, but sacred and cherished prizes I have had.

I have self-sabotaged.

I have risen above.

I have led the way.

Stupid choices I have made that led me to severe and irrevocable consequences.

I have shamed.

I have inspired.

I have inflicted.

Defended many friends through my days with a fiery passion and loyalty.

I have been loved.

I have been loathed.

I have been misunderstood.

For others I have hidden shame, cleaned up literal and figurative messes, sacrificed, mothered, and told the difficult truth.

I have comforted.

I have faltered.

I have refreshed.

I have stood by the sides of those I love through deaths, failures, new beginnings, endings, celebrations, and successes.

I have thought.

I have dreamed.

I have believed.

No matter the failure or struggle, I survive; not because I have a plan, but because I move forward.

I have fear.

I have pride.

I have strength.

Though it has cost me dearly, I remain the same; able to be read like a book, to learn more simply turn the page.

I have layers.

I have depth.

I have clarity.

Kindred to a time not of my own; my soul remains old, my mind remains open, my heart remains young, and my life remains hungry for more.

I am, as I am, and now, I have been heard; and you, well, you have learned.

PERSPECTIVE

It's sort of funny
That epiphany of the obvious
When logic somehow reaches
The heart
How the advice freely given
Is openly taken
By one and the self

Anger and pity are vile
Creatures of evil
And though we each possess an amount
The control we give it
Truly lies within our own
Choices
I choose freedom
And freedom cannot exist
Within the shadows of negativity

I've faced demons
Some of my own creation
Others of others
And instead of the break I once sought
I await the next
Because I'm ready
And I choose the future

All I have survived prepared me
For tomorrow and the next
Instead of seeing the worn and the weathered
I'm happy to embrace the idea
That I've been bred for something more

Hearts do not grow simply for growing
Compassion does not appear from nothing
My days past have nurtured these both

From sorrow can grow beautiful things
Trials can fertilize greatness

So I give my love freely
Knowing there are those that may not appreciate it
There are those, in fact, who may abuse it
Kindness I genuinely shall share
Knowing there are those that may overlook it
There are those, in fact, that do not want it

And challenges I shall meet with a running start
Because I can and because I am
Because I don't choose to believe
I know that I've been bred for something
Amazing

CREATING

Should our thoughts meet
In the exchanges of a quiet day
What sort of epiphany might we birth
If our hearts spent a moment within the other
Amidst the chaos of our lives
What sort of connected understanding would that invoke
Had our pasts walked alongside the other's
Within a history bred deep and long
What sort of home might the comfort of one another's company arouse
Could you dream my dreams as I dream yours
On a lonely night warmed by possibilities
What sort of inspiration could that ignite
Would our souls choose to embrace and lock
Drawn by a force undisputed by our world
What sort of kindred existence shall it design
I behold the beauty and wonder before me
Join me on this journey and we will discover the possibilities together
Meeting our potential is not a question, but a reality
Spent my life waiting and preparing
Now I embark to begin my creating

LOOK

What is contained in a look
At which point do the words which refuse to pass
Translate in another way

Curiosity demands but a second more, a second look
Pity may draw our glance to the solid ground
Dreams of something more fly our eyes high

The heart will lock you in, refusing to allow a pull away
Spread of happiness, pain, love
Contagious fear, anger wistfulness
All exchanged within the moment

Fleeting seconds that pass between two
Sharing something likely of
Chance
Awkward
Blissful
Communicative
Elements woven together

Peak of the exchange approaches and so many possibilities present

Each moment we make choices
Defining and directing our paths
To a point of crossing, merging, or straying further from one another

So much hinders on the moments of our shared looks
At that briefest slice of time what will drive our fate

What shall be
When we share a look

THEY ALL ASK…

The question I'm asked
Sometimes embedded on the face of another
Tip toeing through my mind at the worst of times
Whispers between friends and family
Puzzlement unexplored by many I'm known to
Words posed by any that brush past my heart
Why?
How?
It's unbelievable, I'm told
So surprising, for sure
A reason hidden, there must somehow be

Luck is questioned
Chance and fate ignored
All cashed in for shrouds of doubt
Quests for proving the truth untrue

In all the forms of your questions and wonderings
Little cracks form in the rock of confidence behind which I've hidden
Breaking free may be painful and necessary

But then again, I know
They'll ask and they'll wonder
Why?
How?

Thus the cycle shall repeat
Until the path is destroyed
And a greater adventure begins

WORDS

Words
Cheap costly things
Intricately simple
Heavy and soft
Somethings that make and beak
Moments and people
Conveyors of meaning and purpose
Suffocates at the surface
Reliefs at the end

ART OF LIFE

We are a collage of the people we have met

Artwork within our power with which we powerlessly become

This is how we shape ourselves and pass the power and responsibility of what we become to others

Until we find pride and then it is our own, but should misery befall our lives the blame shall be upon the artists and never upon the canvas

The brush passed from self to another, bristles composed of the fibers of my being and those rooted in the fibers from which I was birthed

Handle crafted and shaped by God so as not to fit into the hand of just anyone

While forcefully gripped anyone may wield the brush, however only the fated will comfortably compose upon the canvas

Marks of violence and betrayal will not abandon the canvas

Anyone may seize the brush when I drop it down should it behoove them

Forgetting to muster the strength, for it takes a mighty amount, to hold the brush until another may come to add their flair

My brush may fall, become dirty, and need to be cleansed of its past adventures

Continuing to evolve and change, while nothing is ever removed and only covered, the canvas will only become its intended masterpiece the moment my last breath passes from my lips

It will be then, only then, that finished it will be, the

Art of Life

RELATIONSHIPS CHANGE AND NOTHING IN LIFE IS PERMANENT

Relationships change as people evolve and experiences are thrust upon us.

This cannot be denied and though it is not always the warm and fuzzy thought sought after by so many, it is the truth.

Someone, though wise and compassionate he is not, bestowed upon me some very sage advice once upon time. He told me,

"Nothing in life is permanent."

I find myself often repeating it over and over again. Though I'm not always as accepting or understanding of this simple yet profound statement, I cannot deny the truth it holds.

So, as nothing is truly permanent,

relationships change and are not permanent.

This change can become a roller coaster,

it can be the growth of something strong or beautiful,

and at other times it can be confusing and disheartening.

The most intriguing aspect of this idea is that while

nothing is permanent and relationships change,

they are all a choice.

We choose whether or not we have particular relationships in our lives, we choose the deepness of the relationships in our lives,

and we choose whether or not to

nurture a relationship.

How do we go about choosing the individuals with which we will share nothing,

share merely minuscule moments, or

share all of who we are?

Could this be an operation of instinct and gut feeling, something perhaps that

we are chemically driven to do with one individual as opposed to another?

Or is this something that is shaped by our experiences of trust, mistrust, loyalty, and fallacy of friendships?

As much as I want to say that I operate through wisdom of choice,

I find myself leaning more toward the idea that I am drawn to trust or not trust particular individuals by gut and instinct.

Is my judgement and instinct always correct?

Of course I'm sometimes wrong,

but I'm more often correct.

Perhaps the more important question I should be asking myself is

how often I listen to those instincts.

I have to wonder what the theories of others are when it comes to this very topic of relationships and change.

I particularly find myself curious when it comes to the theories of those with whom I share my life.

What makes a friendship tick and what exactly allows for there to be chemistry of trust and companionship in a friendship?

There are some people that can be instant friends and others that take time to build a closeness. Are particular individuals in possession of a personality that acts as a magnet to others like themselves or a particular other kind of personality?

Why does friendship grow more easily between some than it does between others?

I have found this in my own life, where friendship slowly crawls

along without my understanding of its stunted growth while I also experience

friendships that blossom quickly with roots shooting deep into the ground for a fantastic foundation.

I find myself mulling over the questions

of why

I have certain relationships in my life,

why some relationships are not the way I wish that they were,

and why

relationships are sometimes so much easier for me with some people than with others.

I don't quite have the answers, except that relationships change and that nothing in life is permanent.

What this will mean for my relationships with friends and family can only be told over time as

things inevitably change.

A TRUE LOVE POEM

It comes and it goes
Some days it mostly goes and others it mostly comes
The flash of your face
The sound of your name
The memories in my heart
The driving me to be a better person
And they envelope me in sadness and grief
This journey of healing, a journey of life without you
Is so much harder than I imagined
And I feared the difficulties it would present
The average cannot comprehend
Counterparts and equals unable to fathom or grasp
Be it ignorance or jealousy or apathy
Your title did not reflect your position
More, so much more
A uniqueness to the connection, the bond, the love
Those who did not witness or share in our love
Exist eluded by the importance, the dependence
By name you were Papa, you are my Papa
But you were so much more
You set the standard for men in my life
The first few years of my life you were my main man, my hero, my protector, my rock
You gave me love, kindness, gentleness, playfulness, balance
You taught me the value of family, of honor, or hard work, of sacrifice, of faith, of God
Life is scary without you here and at many times everything feels so hollow
It's quieter, with not as many corny jokes, no war and police stories, and less reminders of high expectations

Your wisdom remains, imprinted upon my heart, encased by your beautiful love
You told me I made you proud
I know you knew what you meant and still mean to me
Your love still fills my heart
But I still cry, I still hurt, and I still need you
Perhaps I always will
So until we are together again, just until then, I continue to carry a piece of your soul inside my own
So that I may survive, drawing from your strength
So that I might honor you by being a reflection of how amazing you were

THE LEGACY OF CHAILEM

Perpetuating questions
Love - choice or obligation
Beliefs of either disintegrate
In the fires of trial and tribulation
Where truth and core are revealed
Once the mask and created facade melt away
Venom and beauty exposed
Suspicions confirmed
Love: actions, feelings, expression
Separately one united by the existence
All a choice
The selfishness of your nature
Reveals the reality
Always, it is a choice
While treatment by some is of obligation
To create the sums of condition of self-benefit
Those that have chosen a love without condition
Have a peace and beauty unattainable by the tainted souls
That spit venom of conditions and spout excuses of selfishness
Assumptions proven clear and true, no satisfaction in the disappointment of being right
Hope for a shard of light within you melts into an angry death
Disgusting and distasteful, disposable half cares expressed on a whim
We all now know
Who you have chosen to be
Perhaps who you've remained to be
And the love you have chosen to withhold
Forsaking our love and hope to fulfill the selfishness of the others

While the fury may rise in us
The poison present within and around you was self-
induced

a dreAm

Today I mourn a dream
From which I was vehemently awoken
Shockwaves of reality washed upon a
Hopeful heart now left to drown
Desires of the soul whispered into
Etchings upon my mind
Manifesting as a mere dream
A tease of something that
Might, could, should, will
Be
Salivating to savor a single moment
Satisfaction for a hungry emptiness
Reaching out in the dark crevices of a dream
My inner truth speaks to me
Shall I listen
Or prod forward ignorantly
Reality will reap the answer

WHAT ARE YOU?

I knew I was different when people would come up to me in the supermarket and ask me what I was.

It started young when friends amongst strangers would inquire and ask, "Are you adopted?" "You look different, like you don't belong to your family." "Who do you belong to?" "What are you?" "I've been looking at you and…well, I just can't figure you out."

In third grade I got into an argument with a girl, who didn't believe I was Chinese. She told me I looked more Hawaiian. She said my eyes weren't squinty enough to be Chinese.

In 8th grade the girl who was now best friends with my ex-best friend would walk past my locker and yell out "Chink!" I had to go home and ask my mother what that meant.

In 11th grade my boyfriend broke up with me because his dad didn't want him dating an Asian girl.

White to the Chinese family and Chinese to the white family.

No place to belong.

Identity forsaken and no place amongst the labels.

"Oh, college applications, hmm…well, no dear, you cannot select more than one. Why don't you just choose 'other'? You seem to fit best in that category."

I was told to be Asian when it suited me best and to be White when that suited me best.

But, really, am I Caucasian or Asian?

"You're Chinese? You don't really look like it."

When my Chinese grandmother passed away, my Ngng, I looked whiter than usual. My family members would talk about the "Lofans" that came to visit and pay their respects…those white people, my people.

"I can tell, you're mixed with something, aren't you? What are you?" To many of our Chinese friends and family members I was different.

"I bet you're smart, you're Chinese." And the pressure mounted from there, I hadn't realized that Asian = must be smart and good at everything, those Asians, my people.

My sister has a different father and we have ten long years between us. People ask her why her sister looks Asian when she is clearly not.

"What are you?"

Dating, haha…oh, dating. I totally tried the online thing. Yep, wow, what a nightmare. You have to select your race on there. No one likes "Other"… but if I put "Asian" I attracted the Asian-obsessed and if I put "White" people just didn't believe me because I looked different and they would ask, "What are you?"

"So, you're different…huh, so, uh, then, what are you?"

To this day I get stopped in the grocery store, in waiting rooms, by kids and adults, nothing holds them back…they all want to know and so they all ask me:

"What are you?"

Haha, you want to know what I am? I'm human. I'm American. I'm Chinese, I'm French-Canadian, I'm Polish, and I'm here. I'm unique, I'm strong and I'm wonderful. I have feelings and I have thoughts. I contribute to society, and I am not some object to be categorized, weighed, measured, and in need of justification.

So, what am I? I'm someone who would never question you, what you are.

ABOUT THE AUTHOR

This is Melissa Moy's second poetic collection to be published. Her first collection was written over the course of a couple of years where she experienced a difficult time in her life. *Mosaic of my Mind* is a collection of poetry written over the course of just under twenty years. Moy penned these poems beginning in high school and into her thirties. She held on to the poems that, she felt, moved her most deeply and it is here that they make their home.

Melissa Moy graduated from Oakland University Magna Cum Laude with a degree in Elementary Education and endorsement in ELA in 2012. Moy completed the five year program in three and a half years. Months after graduation Moy began teaching English and Reading at Boulan Park Middle School in Troy, MI. She also established and coaches the school's current competitive forensics program. Moy obtained a MA in Educational Psychology from Eastern Michigan University in 2017.

Her enthusiasm for learning and growing as an educator is only matched by her corny and sarcastic humor. Moy also dedicates time and love to rescuing Chihuahuas with Chihuahua Rescue & Transport, a national rescue. Working to support a very dear cause, CURED, Dodge does what she can to help raise funds and awareness in hopes of finding a cure for Eosinophilic Diseases.

Writing under her maiden name, Melissa Moy, she has published this second poetic collection and Spring of 2018 brought forth her first children's picture book.

thank you for taking the time to peruse the ponderings of my pen

~

it would mean a great deal to me if you would take a moment and review this poetic collection

… until next time

Made in the USA
Columbia, SC
21 November 2023

26858630R00085